God's Will Health, Healing and Wholeness

Pastor Janet Stanfield

PREFACE

I thank God for giving me the opportunity to write this book. If ever there was a time that a book of this magnitude and gravity was needed, it is now. The Lord ministered to me that too many of his people are dying unnecessarily and prematurely due to sickness and disease, and unaware of the fact that Father God needed them to complete their assigned God ordained mission on earth.

Please note that you are not an afterthought with God; for too long sickness and disease has trespassed and ravished the body of believers; it has no place and no right because of the blood covenant between Father God and his children.

Further, He has a glorious plan for your life! He alone makes it possible for you to stay in the Earth and achieve that plan by being whole, spirit, soul, and body! We are redeemed from the curse of the law because Christ was made a curse for us (Galatians 3:13); which is inclusive of poverty, sickness, and spiritual death; and because sickness falls in that category, we as people of God must know and exemplify our position on this subject.

God has already given a clear and precise position; seemingly, we have not heard what the Spirit has spoken to the Church. "Yes," he has spoken, and is still speaking to this day through his Prophets, Apostles, Teachers, Evangelist, Pastors, and of course the people of God. Also, God is perpetually blowing the horn of the gospel message "By whose stripes ye were healed;" some have tried to drown out the sound, even the Ecclesia who is supposed to truly believe the message of faith.

Paul tells us to declare the whole counsel of God. If we do not declare healing for humanity and the entirety of man: body, soul, and spirit; we have missed the mark. God promised to fulfill the number of our days in order for us to finish the work he has called us to do. I believe we as the body of Christ do not teach this enough. The Bible declares: "Jesus went through all the towns and villages, teaching in their synagogues, proclaiming the good news of the kingdom and healing every sickness and disease among the people (Matthew 9:35), NIV."

Therefore, our job is not just to preach a half truth, but the whole truth of the gospel message. We know how to receive Christ in our lives for the most part. However, do we know how to partake of healing in the same manner? This must be taught simultaneously; nothing must be left to chance, all must be fulfilled. The world must see and know a Jesus who heals not just the soul and spirit, but the body as well.

THIS GOSPEL MUST BE PREACHED!!

INTRODUCTION

To Achieve Your Dream: Do the Impossible

I am Pastor Janet Stanfield and I believe God has a great plan for your life! Believe it or not, you are not on planet Earth just to exist. God has a divine plan and a purpose exclusively for you because your God ordained destiny is the most essential thing in your life!

Growing up, on occasion I would hear mom and dad speak of God. I was totally oblivious to God's plan and purpose for me until I became very ill and was afraid of dying. I began to search the Bible for answers and had a manifestation of Truth; I found out that God wanted me well in every aspect of my being; spirit, soul and body, WOW! My confession immediately changed. I said to myself: "YES, God really wants me to complete my destiny on earth with total wellness."

It became increasingly clear to me that I am a woman fearfully and wonderfully made with purpose, plan, and destiny! I could not afford to die.

After the awakening, I determined I needed to know God on a personal basis. Knowing God in that way involved developing a relationship with God by way of consistently and persistently reading and meditating on God's living Word. That in association with the assistance of faithful blood-bought saints whose gift of presence generated new life, brought me to full knowledge of Christ. I would not have made it without divine intervention, but I also determined and confessed it was time for me to live and not die!

This book reminds us how much God wants his people well and the price he paid for us to be well in our whole being. As I was writing this book, I asked God to cover my entire family and shield them from all manner of sickness and disease; to date, they have not been chronically sick a day in their lives. For this, I give all the glory to God. According to Ephesians 6:12: "We wrestle not against flesh and blood but against principalities, against powers, against the rulers of the darkness of this world, against spiritual wickedness in high places." Therefore, we must always be alert and sober in prayer (for ourselves, our families, and the world), looking for His goodness.

I believe that everyone who reads this book is healed. If you are sick, you are on your way to recovery from any type of sickness and disease. Some will be healed and see the manifestation instantly, while some manifestations of wholeness are a process. No matter the process, Christ's endgame is always the same: health, healing, and wholeness!

I pray and believe this book will reach the audience it is supposed to reach and

in reading this book you will understand
and know the love of God that surpasses
all understanding.

DEDICATION

I dedicate this book to my loving husband Clarence; without his presence, powerful prayers, and love, this book would not have been possible.

I also dedicate my words to my mom, the late Beulah M. White, to my children, Akela, Clarence, and Kelali, as well as my grandchildren Moriah and Selali.

Finally, I dedicate this text to my future generations and to those who will take time to read this book and embody and believe in the healing power of Jesus the Christ. It is God's will that "none in Zion shall say they are sick" (Isaiah 33:24).

TABLE OF CONTENTS

CHAPTER 1

Healing Is For EVERYONE

"My people are destroyed for lack of knowledge."

The year was 1975, the month was May, and I was so excited about the prospect of going to the prom. This was what all girls looked forward to during this time and season if you were at least sixteen and in the eleventh grade. I was excited for my "coming out." Coming out was a way for all the girls around my age to feel like they were dressing up as a grown woman for the first time. I was so excited that year I could not wait to try on my dress and show the world what I looked like at my most glamorous. I still remember the way the gown looked. It was peach colored with ruffles all over. Mom told me "either you get the dress or the class ring. You will not be able to afford both." So of course, I chose the dress. You know how we are as teenagers, it's all about instant gratification. I was no different. I coveted the dress and nothing else would do other than me having it. I wanted the man of my dreams (or so I thought) to admire me. But unbeknownst to me, there was something in the shadows lurking around to steal my joy. Satan always walks about seeking whom he may devour (1Peter 5:7).

Throughout that time, I was losing weight rapidly, but I attributed it to a few skipped meals. I was not watchful and did not know how to be. I did not know God the way I know him now and really was not the least bit interested in knowing Him. Mom and Dad knew Him and that was enough for me. The critical point is that I did not realize how my spiritual health and my physical health were linked in ways that had real consequences for my life.

"Remember your Creator in the days of your youth, before the days of trouble come and the years approach and you will say, "I find no pleasure in them." (Eccl. 12:1).

I just kept moving and trying to get ready for the task at hand. I was a self-centered teenager focused on enjoying the days ahead. Nothing else really mattered to me.

I was also busy with my schoolwork and cheerleading. I kept noticing the weight I was losing but did nothing to address it. Eventually, I became very ill. I did not want to tell mom about it because I knew that meant giving up my busy schedule and fun. I lacked the perspective to see that cheerleading and the prom were nothing compared to my health. Finally, I could not ignore my condition any longer. One day I came home from school and was so exhausted I could not stand up. My mom immediately told me to lay down and get some rest. When I awoke the next morning, my condition had not changed. Even now I can remember how bad I felt and how terrified I was. I did not feel like myself and I could not even stand on my own two feet. I became bedridden.

Throughout that time, I missed school. I missed hanging out with my friends and just talking the normal every day talk for girls at the age of sixteen (Boys!). We paid the doctor's office a visit. They could not diagnose the problem but gave me some pills and sent me home. The next day I felt there was no change. I began to worry and so did mom.

Even though I did not know God the way I know Him now, I attended church regularly; healing was never mentioned, only confessing your sins and being saved from eternal damnation (Hell's Fire). I was only interested in not going to Hell and not interested in being healed when I was sick, I just did not want to go to Hell; I didn't know God the King in all the Earth was interested in me being healed from any type of sickness; I just thought He did not want me to die and go to Hell, I asked myself: "Why would He want me to be delivered from Sickness after all, wasn't Heaven enough?"

We were not taught to look forward and experience the joys of heaven on earth and that we should expect to be healed in the "now" because it is part of the blood covenant between God and his inheritance. Healing was for the "pie in the sky and the sweet by and by" not for this life or this time.

"My people are destroyed for lack of knowledge." (Hosea 4:6).

My mom evidently had experienced Gods' healing hand one time or another. She called on her best friend and faith partner and told her to immediately pray for me. She prayed, but I grew worse and not better. Sound familiar?

The Bible proclaims in Luke 8:44: "that a woman who was subject to bleeding for twelve years came up behind him [Jesus] and touched the edge of his cloak, and immediately her bleeding stopped." No one could heal her (Luke 8:43 NIV). Like this woman, I went to many doctors in my home town, but they could not pin point the problem. I laid there day in and day out trying to trust the God my mom and dad knew. I was about to learn a very powerful lesson that would stay with me for the rest of my life.

Not knowing that in God's beautiful plan of salvation, healing is for every one of us in every area of our lives spirit, soul, and body. I felt relief in not just my body, but also in my mind and spirit. Further, when there is a relief in the soul of a man, there is also relief in the body.

The Bible boldly proclaims: "Beloved I wish above all things that thou mayest prosper and be in health even as thy soul prospers (3 John 1:1-2). God's plan is for his children to be whole in every area of their lives. He did not come just to save us but to rescue us from Satan's dominion. Your body is as equally important to God as the salvation of your soul and spirit are. God's plan of salvation for man is holistic and inclusive, meaning that man is complete, "adorned with every Christian grace and wanting nothing."

Our bodies have been rescued; God declared in the Old Testament "if thou wilt diligently hearken to the voice of the Lord thy God, and wilt do that which is right in his sight, and will give ear to his commandments, and keep all his statues, I will put none of these diseases upon thee, which I have bought upon the Egyptians: for I am the Lord that healeth thee (Exodus 15:26)."If you study this verse, you will find that it was never God who put or caused sickness and disease; conversely it was because God's people did not obey his word. Every sin and error has a just recompense of reward. It was never God's will for his people to suffer the punishment of this world; the punishment of sin is always from the god of this world, not Father God that is why Jesus died to take away the punishment of sin and sickness.

I charge you to never accept sickness and disease another day in your life! I found out the importance of knowing my rights and privileges in Christ. Once I put in my mind and spirit that I would not be sick another day in my life I decided to stay well. I decided that I would fight the devil at every turn and if I had the slightest symptom in my body of sickness I would jump on top of it right then and there with the Word of God, not letting it linger or fester. I made up in my mind that I would resist the devil at his onslaught!

You must do the same if you plan to stay well and take God at his word.

The covenant in Isaiah 54:10 declares "The mountains shall depart and the hills be removed but my kindness will not depart from thee, neither shall the covenant of my peace be removed, saith the Lord that hath mercy on thee." This passage of Scripture immediately informs me that because of God's unyielding love; his love and kindness will not abandon me and that he is not the one tempting me to believe in being sick, I knew that above all, God wanted me well and that His will for me is "Health, Healing, and Wholeness".

I can truly say for the many years that I've been standing on the healing Word of God I haven't had a need to go to the doctor other than for a checkup obeying the word of God as it says: "prove all things" (1 Thessalonians 5:21).

I did not say I did not have aches or pain. Believe you me, you will have the opportunity to resist the devil just as you do anything else in your Christian walk; but when you become aware and know that Jesus bore your sickness and pain; you will stand with confidence resisting the devil and he will flee from you. Remember, when the doctor gives you a bad report you have the word of God to utilize against all manner of sickness and disease, this is your God given right and a divine privilege, resist it and stand in victory.

CHAPTER 2

God Wants You Well

The one thing in my life I did not realize in my formative years was that God had a predestined plan for my life and that in order to achieve my predetermined plan; God wanted me well! I needed to be well to discover and move toward fulfillment of the plan God has expressly for me on planet earth. As I laid in the bed that morning thinking and looking over my life, I began to rehearse all the things I had accomplished in my life and discovered I had done little or nothing; certainly nothing epic. However, I soon realized I was only fifteen going on sixteen and to the contrary, I had lived a pretty full life. God had another plan; this plan would enlighten the understanding of my eyes and I would see more clearly than I had ever seen before; above all, it was not the will of God for me to be sick, not now, not ever. Further, God wanted me to be cognizant of the fact that because of the fall of man, sickness and disease inhabited the earth, not because God was flawed, but because man had disobeyed God and fell from Grace opening himself up to all manner of sickness and disease.

For man to be sick was never God's plan, but I felt God had a lesson to teach me and by the grace of God, I would learn it come hell or high water! However, I did not know the devil also had a plan and that was to destroy me before Gods preordained plan could take effect in my life.

It is my belief that when God has a plan for your life, that plan was in effect before the foundation of the world. Jeremiah 29:11 tells us clearly, "I know the plans

I have for you saith the Lord, plans of peace and not of evil to give you an expected end." Again, I had an epiphany; God wanted me well more than I did.

It's crazy, the things we think about when we think we are leaving and packing it up. Who would come to my funeral? Where would they place me? What would they even say about me? I knew I was pretty nice but would they tell the truth, you know we always have a higher opinion of ourselves than anyone else other than God. Those things did not matter. But, that goes to show you how we think when we have not totally surrendered to Him.

One day came and another went and I didn't feel any better. I must have gone to every doctor in the county, but to no avail. I still felt the same. One night my dad came over to see me. He and my mom were not together during this horrible time in my life but they were cordial to one another so he was allowed to come to the house to see us. I won't go into detail; that's another story within itself. All I wanted was relief.

One should know that sickness and disease is not the plan of God for your life because it sucks the life out of everything around you. Your energy, your finances, your joy, your focus. Everything that is good. Sickness has nothing to do with life. Its' main focus is death, death at work in the body. This is why it is so important for sickness to be eradicated. My dad came and stood over my bed and anointed me in oil and prayed for me. The Bible declares: "is any sick among you? Let him call for the Elders of the church; and let them pray over him anointing him with oil in the name of the Lord" (James 5:14).

My dad was an Elder in the church and he took the Word of God and applied it to my situation. I was so sick, I could not hold my head up to see him. I now admit, I felt a little safer with just him being there, after all he was a man of the cloth. Many days had passed and I was in my bedroom. I would hear conversations about me and my sickness from my family. I don't know if they knew I could hear them talking, but the prognosis was not good. Some even thought to themselves, "what if she dies what would we do?"

I knew my family loved me, but that kind of talk sure didn't help matters any. I needed some hope and the only hope I could cling to was the word of God. I had a Bible and it became my best friend. I kept it in bed with me. My mom told me to quote the twenty-third division of Psalms day and night and that's exactly what I did.

Even though mom had experienced many trials and tribulations throughout her life; I knew that no matter what happened or didn't happen. Mom loved

God, and through her unyielding love and faith in God, mom managed to muster up enough strength and courage to keep trusting in him. Although I'm sure at times she felt abandoned, so did I.

I always heard that God was a good God, but where was He in my time of need? Did He really want me well or was it to prove a point that He could take me anytime. He wanted to. Whenever He got ready to? Further, this was my thinking: "did I have any say so in my life at all, or was I just to lay there and figure my number had come up and that was that?" That's probably what got me in that predicament in the first place. My thinking.

I remember my mom had to take many days off of work because of the illness I went through. One thing I learned about sickness and disease is that it not only robs you of your life, but your finances., etc.

All I knew is that I did not want to die before I had lived out my allotted time on Earth. I felt I was too young to die. I also knew there was something extraordinary about leaving planet earth before it was my time to leave. Proverbs 18:14 states: "A man's spirit will sustain him in his infirmity." I had just begun to live.

I missed the prom that year. I was too sick to go so I watched my twin sister go to the prom with her high school sweetheart while I laid in the bed and could hardly move.

Somehow and some way I had to defeat what was holding me back. This thing that held me captive. It was no fun being sick. I was so determined to be well and feel well again in my body that I wanted to defy the odds. I asked myself: "How can I feel good again how and how can I feel alive again?"

One of the many gifts that God has given the human spirit is perseverance. I knew

God empowered me with the spirit of perseverance because I was too sick and too weak to accomplish this on my own, but I certainly wanted to try. All God needs is someone who is willing to do what he commands and I then knew God needed me in the Earth, and I wanted so desperately to be used by Him. One must have a will to live and not die "for it is He who works in us to will and to do of his good pleasure (Philippians 2:13)." No one wants to die. It is something about man that craves life, I believe God put that in man's human spirit. Man has an insatiable will to lie and to thrive because the breath of God is within every man; therefore, it is part of the human experience that man has an unquenchable desire for life and perhaps that's why death is never welcomed.

There are many reasons God wants us well, but the main reason I believe is not only to give God the Glory, but also, to demonstrate Satan's defeat in the earth.

Sickness and disease is an enemy to the church. When the body of the church really grasps this, we will refuse to be sick. We will no longer tolerate sickness and disease to operate another day in our lives, "by whose stripes ye were healed (1 Peter 2:24)."

CHAPTER 3

I Believe I Receive

"My words are spirit and they are life."

The most important and powerful aspect of healing that I really needed to know is that by "faith" I was already healed before the healing manifested in my body. Then and only then would I walk in the newness of the abundant life, infused with His healing power. I still felt badly, but I knew what God's word said about my healing and being healed. I knew without the word of God that there would be no healing. God's word is life, "keep me alive as you have promised" (Psalm 119:25 NIRV); Jesus said: "my words are spirit and they are life," this life that emanates from God's word is the defense we have against demons and spiritual powers; God and His word are one.

Receiving healing or anything from God has to do with a fixed eye on the word of God; "if your eye be single your whole body will be full of light." Keep your eye on what God said about healing. Find scriptures on what God has to say about your situation and spend time meditating on it. Rehearse it over and over again to yourself. See yourself well. See yourself doing what you could not do while you are feeling sick. Put this word in front of your eyes and in your ears because the word of God is health and strength to your flesh.

The Bible teaches us that his word is his medicine. In the book of Proverbs in chapter four, it states: "God's word is health to our flesh and strength to our bones." The word of God is His life and light or His energy so to speak. It lives in you. Allow it to go down to the joints and marrow so it can do its work, your only responsibility is to believe and receive what God says, and the only way you can do that is to meditate on the word of healing day and night.

I have studied many books on healing. I have read what other people have to say about it. The most important thing I learned about healing is when you experience healing for yourself no one can take that experience away from you. Experiences teach us how to walk with God.

I don't believe in sickness and disease. I know that is a bold statement, but you can't believe in something you are trying to get rid of. You must doubt that sickness can live in your body and believe that His word is greater than the sickness that is trying to take residence in your body. Jesus made the statement: "except you believe you cannot enter into the Kingdom of God." Healing comes from God's Kingdom not from this worlds' system. The world can cover the symptoms but it cannot heal; asks any doctor, he will tell you: "we can cover the symptoms because this is what medicine does, but we cannot heal you, only God can do that."

Every time I was healed or relieved from symptoms of sickness, it was not from a doctor. It came through the words of our Lord and Savior Jesus Christ. Do not get it twisted I am not telling you to throw away your medicine. I go to my primary care physician to get checked out once a year. Jesus said "prove all things." I just believe the word of God, because when it comes to choosing between the two; I choose God's word every time. Believe me, many people would be dead if it were not for the doctors. Even Christians, because they would not choose God's word instead of their symptoms. You will side with one or the other. "Which will you choose? God or Mammon?" Jesus said "either you will love one or hate the other."

I looked up the word "receive" in the Merriam Webster Dictionary and it says: "to hold as truth or to take"; I like the word "take" better because you have the opportunity to decide what you want to do. No one can take your healing for you, it must be acquired by you and only you to get the results you desire. Jesus stated: "according to your faith so be it done unto you." It takes faith to receive and believe the word of God.

Believing is different than receiving in biblical terms. Whenwe believe on biblical terms, we hold it as already being done because of NOW FAITH." The difference is holding fast to the "NOW;" whether we hold fast or not, it does not change the word of God. It is still effective and it will produce the results we need, if we are obedient to it.

CHAPTER 4

The True Meaning Of God's Healing Power

"In sickness a man's spirit will sustain him."

I did not study to know the true meaning of God's healing power until I believed I was gravely ill. Even then; the only reason I wanted to be healed is because, I felt badly. Not because God wanted me to walk in true healing and divine health in every area of my life.

As I was lying in the bed, I began to think: "I missed out on one of the most important events in my life," and I began to weep bitterly. The closest person to me at that time was my twin sister, and she and her boyfriend (now her husband) had just walked out the door. Taking with them my dreams and aspirations of going to the prom with the young man of my dreams. I could not help but ask God "why," I just couldn't fathom or process it all.

Sickness robs us of everything good and "every perfect gift" (James 1:17) that God has for us. It causes us to miss out on the best things in life. Further, as I laid there, I began to think about the good time they would have without me and all the people that would ask my whereabouts. I especially thought about how the young man that was supposed to escort me to the prom felt after looking forward to going and could not attend due to my illness.

Daylight finally came and I was extremely saddened that I had missed out on all the things I thought was fun; not knowing that God had a plan for my life that was so much greater than a dance; but you know teenagers, everything is an emergency and if what we planned did not work out, that was deemed catastrophic. I felt the same way in my body, but my spirit felt a little better because the prom was over and I no longer had to dread missing that. It had become a thing of the past.

I remember getting out of bed that morning and sitting on the floor playing a game called "Bobby Jacks," and I somehow felt better. Remember, previously I learned that "in sickness a man's spirit will sustain him" (Proverbs 18:14). I believe my spirit was sicker than my body. I was deeply depressed about not being able to go to the prom. I felt better after the prom was over. Sometimes it's our spirit that's sick, and it transfers to the body and mind.

Jesus said: "As a man thinketh in his heart so is he" (Proverbs 23:7). I was totally unaware of this fact at the time, but it is very true. We have to change our thought process according to Romans 12:2: "Do not conform to the pattern of this world, but be transformed by the renewing of your mind."

After the prom was over, I literally started feeling better; I didn't feel completely well, but I felt better. The first thing mom asked each day when she came in the door was: "how was I feeling?" I felt relieved on the day that I was able to give mom some good news.

Throughout the process of all of this, my being ill and feeling "better," I learned that God did not only want to heal my body, but He had a far greater aim for me; God wanted to heal me body, soul, and spirit!

CHAPTER 5

The Heart Will Keep the Body

"And the very God of peace sanctify you wholly; and I pray God your whole spirit and soul and body be preserved blameless unto the coming of our Lord Jesus Christ."

When waiting for the manifestation of ones' healing, even your own, in between believing and receiving, you must remember to know how to hold on to your healing. You must safeguard it after you receive it. The enemy of our soul loves to rob us of every blessing God has freely given us.

Further, while in between believing and receiving your healing. You must also keep in mind that feelings have nothing to do with the promises of God made to you through the word of God. Although you may immediately begin to feel better; it is important to note, sometimes you must walk out on your faith without feeling or seeing any change.

The Bible tells us to hold on to what thou hast; when you have received your healing the enemy of your soul will definitely try and talk you out of your blessing. You will have to "cast down imaginations and every high thing that exalts itself against the knowledge of God and bring every thought captive to the obedience of Christ." (2 Corinthians 10:5).

Paul knew about bringing his mind into obedience. He talked about being shipwrecked, stoned, and left for dead, but he never complained about being sick. "I wonder why?" I believe Paul resolutely knew in his mind that sickness was not part of God's great plan for his people.

When you become aware of the fact that God has spoken from his holy word, you also understand that this is the reason we continue to stand. Knowing that the foundation of God stands assure. When you learn to stand on the word of God for your healing. You will learn to rest on everything else that God has promised you. The promises of God according to 2nd Corinthians 1:20: "For all the promises of God in him are yea, and in him Amen." I encourage you to continue having done all to stand, keep standing.

I believe when we learn to take a firm stand, a believing stand on our God given authority in His word. The devil gets tired of attacking the same avenue. I did not say he gives up. But, because you have taken that ground it is not so easy for him to deceive you any more in that area.

When you learn to hold your ground, it becomes easier for you to do so especially when it comes to healing. When you walk out in faith on God's word it becomes your first response not your last. This is how you drive sickness and disease out of your body. Resist sickness and disease at its onslaught. Don't wait to investigate. Resist it then. Not later. Anything that is foreign and not of God's word should be cast down immediately. Not allowing it to have a foothold in your life.

The longer sickness and disease stays and builds a trench. The harder it is to get it out. This is where watching as well as praying comes in. Although, I speak this from my experience. experience is not the best teacher. Especially when it comes to sickness. The best teacher is the word of God because that is the only remedy. Hold on to God's word and the results will be total victory. "This is the victory that overcomes the world even our Faith."

You cannot teach healing without teaching faith, because faith and healing work in agreement with each other when it comes to believing God's word and in order to hold on to your healing you must walk by faith and not by sight. The enemy of your soul is sure to test you to see if you really believe what you are standing on, but don't take down. Hold your ground and you will definitely feel and know God's word is triumphant in every situation.

In this lifetime, you will have to stand against sickness and disease; not that it will always manifest in your body, but the temptation to giving in to the tempters lies will try and haunt you throughout your life, therefore, you will always have the opportunity to resist him and to stand firm in your faith, and as you hold steady in your faith you will always win.

CHAPTER 6

Hold on To Your Healing

"Take the helmet of salvation, and the sword of the Spirit which is the word of God."

The story of Redemption brought healing to the whole world; absolutely no one was left out, all have a right to the tree of life. God told Adam to go into the garden to conquer and subdue it which meant he had dominion over everything that was in the Garden of Eden; Adam even had dominion over his body, that's why he stayed well until the fall of man. If Adam and Eve had never sinned they would have never gotten sick or known anything about disease, therefore they would have never died physically or spiritually.

Sickness was never a part of God's plan for man. Satan had to deceive man in order for him to fall for the statement "Hath God said" (Genesis 3:1), Satan had to get them to first doubt what God said to them, Satan has not changed his tactics they are still the same. "Did God really say" same thing different disguise. God had already told them they were gods (Psalms 82:6), they were already just like God, but they did not believe it or they would not have been deceived into thinking they were not like God.

In the Book of Isaiah (54:1-5) the "Eagle Eye Prophet," talked about the suffering servant that was "wounded for our transgressions, bruised for our iniquities, the chastisement of our peace was upon him, and with his wounds we are healed!" That's why we need to take heed what we hear; in other words, we need to be careful what we internalize. Our life is in our heart so we need to guard our hearts, because "out of it flow the issues of life" (Proverbs 4:23).

Thank God! We have been redeemed from the curse of the broken law because Christ was made a curse for us. He became the very thing that was killing us; sickness and disease that derives from sin.

Jesus told the woman it was not right or appropriate to take what belonged to the children and give it to the dogs. Why was it the children's bread and not the world's? Simply because Jesus came first to His own and then the world. But Healing belongs to His children because they are His children and they belong to Him. Plain, basic, simple! Jesus died to deliver the whole world from sin and its penalty, but his children have first rights just as your children exclusively have first dibs on everything you own. "But yea

Lord even the dogs eat the crumbs that fall from the masters' table," either this non-covenant woman understood how powerful this covenant was or she was mighty desperate. However, I would go as far as to say she was both, desperate and understood His power and was willing to take what she could get to meet her particular needs or what was sufficient for her at that particular time.

Even today the world uses what His children want, taking advantage of the bountiful privileges that rightfully belong to God's people; the world has a perception and understanding of what they are allowed to do. In the NIV, it states in Matthew 15:27: "that even dogs are allowed to eat the crumbs that fall from the master's table." Can you see the graciousness and willingness of God in that statement?" She had a revelation of who Jesus was better than some believers. She understood that Jesus was gracious and kind or that He could be to her what she believed Him to be. Jesus told her she had great faith because she trusted Him for the little and believed it would be enough for her situation. Isn't it wonderful, that we don't have to settle for the crumbs or the little, when we can have the whole loaf.

Yes!! Healing is fully ours by faith. If we walk by faith and not by sight we can access healing whenever we need it. It is a great part of our inheritance. Christ hath redeemed us from sin to love. Scripture declares that "greater love hath no man than one who would lay down his life for a friend." Yes, He laid down His life for us to have and live redemptions story. The greatest story ever told. You must know that healing is "REDEMPTIONS' STORY," that's a fact, not just the TRUTH. "By whose stripes ye were healed: 1 Peter 2:24."

CHAPTER 7

The Mind: The Control Center to Healing, Health, and Wholeness

"Be ye transformed by the renewing of your mind."

In order to walk in divine healing, you must have the right mind set. Jesus said, "let this mind be in you that was also in Christ Jesus." Your mind set is very important to your well-being and success, especially your body. We have to think soundly in order to walk in healing. Soundly, you may ask? We must think the way God thinks-that takes discipline! Sickness is not a part of God's wisdom because it is the wisdom of God that gives us life and light, "My words are spirit and life" and if you focus on your aches and pains you are focusing on death, which is the wisdom of this world.

What you focus on is what you become. That is why Paul tells us to "cast down imaginations and every high thing that exalts itself against the knowledge of God and to bring our minds into captivity to the obedience of Christ." The mind is the control center of our very existence; therefore, you must be extremely careful what you focus on, because what you focus on is what you become.

Most people's sickness starts within their minds first and foremost, you have to keep your mind elevated and ask yourself: "Whatsoever things are pure, whatsoever things are lovely, praiseworthy, of a good report think on these things," and the peace of God will keep your heart and mind because that mind of yours will keep things from breaking down on you, and that includes your body. When you think correctly your body will respond correctly; it will go in the direction of your last thought. Your brain or mind is your command center, it tells your body what to do. That's why the word of God is so important in our lives; our thoughts will take us places we don't want to go if we think wrongly. Our body will follow suit, that's why we must think the right thoughts.

Take God at His word when it comes to your healing; healing is the children's bread, it belongs to the children. Jesus said it was not right to take the children's bread and give it to dogs. Why? Because healing specifically belongs to the seed of Abraham. It belongs to God's children; it is part and parcel of the gospel message. Whoever and whatever controls the mind controls the body.

You must be careful what you think about and change your thinking. Do not listen to the father of lies, Jesus said he was a liar from the beginning; I am who he says I am and I can do what He says I can do. You cannot walk by your feelings we must walk by faith and not by sight. What we feel does not change God's word; His word does not change, it's immutable. There is no variableness neither shadow of turning in Him.

We must bathe our minds with the word of God in order to get the results He would like for us to get. You must think in line with the word of God. Sickness is not normal In the Kingdom of God; we are in a different Kingdom so we must think in harmony with the Kingdom of light.

Sickness is normal for the world because of what Adam and Eve did; sin was introduced and sickness was its results. The mind must go to its cure, the cross. The control center of our life must be renewed daily with the word of God. The word of GOD is health to our flesh and strength to our bones. The Christian mind must be controlled by the sanctifying work of the Holy Spirit. Yes, the renewed mind "Be ye transformed by the renewing of your mind."

God's word is a dose of medicine to our mind that needs to be taken on a daily basis. Whoever controls the mind controls the body. Set your affections on things above not on things on the earth; we are heavenly beings living on planet earth, our citizenship is in heaven so our minds must be fed from the place that we came from, our nourishment comes from God, He is our living bread of life and living water.

We must be careful what we meditate upon because what we mediate upon is what we become. David talked about meditation and how powerful it had become in his life in Psalms 119:97: "Oh

How love I thy law, I meditate on it all day long." David understood how valuable it was to think and meditate on God's word. The mind receives the engrafted word that saves not just our mind, but our will and emotions, and body as well. The body soul and spirit works together to bring about one harmonious song, and that is the will of God. The body must be in harmony just like our spirit and soul, it must be well. The only way these three can work adequately together is through and by the Spirit.

Can we really live free from sickness through our mind? Yes! Elevate that mind of yours to God's word and sickness will flee, remember, nothing will work unless you bathe your mind with His word. Why, because the word is God.

CHAPTER 8

Talk The Talk

"If you confess with your mouth the Lord Jesus and believe in your heart that God raised Him from the dead, you will be saved."

In order to maintain ones healing you must talk the talk of healing. You will never hold on to your healing if you do not confess what you possess. What I confess I possess. You cannot talk sickness and disease and stay well. "Whatsoever a man confesses with his mouth and believes in his heart" this is what makes him saved, delivered, and made free (Romans 9:10).

You must confess God's word on a daily basis, not one day but every single day of your life, it must become a part of you and the only way this can happen is to say it, say it, and say it! If you say it enough it will get in your heart and you will believe what you are saying. Your tongue as I stated previously has a lot to do with your spirit man. There is a natural man and a spiritual man, these two men co-exist, they work together. It's up to you which one will have preeminence. This is why your tongue is so important, it works by your spiritual man. Whatever you deposit in your spirit will come out in your mouth. "Out of abundance of the heart the mouth will speak" (Luke 6:45) so we must be careful what we have made a deposit on.

That tongue of yours is very important. It was created to perform specific tasks and you are solely responsible for making sure it does the right job, and that is speaking God's word.

God's creative power will connect you with God's ability, if I talk right I will receive right because talking is more than a notion. You must watch what you say. The Bible does not tell us to bridle the tongue for no reason. It can cause the body to run in a direction you do not want it to run in; it may take some time, and then sometimes it may not, but it will catch up with you. Guard your tongue with diligence and caution; your body waits to hear a command from your tongue and it goes right into action. Every tissue, organ, and cell responds to what we say about it or put in it. We will discuss what we put on our tongue later in the book.

James, 3rd chapter says: "the tongue is a deadly poison" but Proverbs says: "the tongue can also promote health," because of the tongues' dual nature, it can work for you or against you. It's your choice. Every part of our body was given to us to accomplish our destiny in the earth and I believe the tongue is the most critical of our members; it shifts our spirit and our flesh. It possesses the power to calm it down, or put it into overdrive. It is such a vital part of our spiritual advancement.

Also, what comes in front of our eyes and enters into our ears is equally important because it enters into our spirit and eventually into our mouths. It's important to surround yourself with people with like mind and like spirit, people saturated with precious faith, especially when you are in warfare over your body. This is when you really need to hear words that are spirit and life. Not words filled with fear and doubt. You can certainly find that on the boob tube, commercials filled with advertisements of numerous medicine for everything other than what your body is being attacked with. Notice I said attacked because it is not yours and it attacks because it is trying to get you to side with it, and agree with it. As soon as you let "I am sick" come out of your mouth you own it. It definitely does not belong to you, especially a believer in Christ Jesus.

Once you have confessed sickness you must go into overdrive and confess the scriptures you know about healing to combat the confessed sickness, don't give the devil a chance to get a foothold in your life. You must clean your spirit daily with the washing of the water, of God's word, so your tongue may speak correctly.

Guard your heart for out of it flows the issues of life. What do you mean clean out my closet? Where did that come from? Your heart is the closet to your soul, it must be kept free from debris so your tongue can agree with the right thing; your tongue will say whatever your closet (heart) is saying at the time, guard your heart, you are custodian over your heart. Be attentive to matters of your heart, do your job and make sure what goes in your heart is good and acceptable and perfect from the original source; God.

Your tongue is the mechanism that God uses to transfer life to your inner-man, which is the heart; your tongue is a useful piece of equipment to get you out of the snare of the devil. When we said earlier that a wise tongue promotes health, we are talking about speaking right words; words that will cause you to live and not die to declare the works of the Lord in the land of the living.

Continually cultivate your tongue to do its duty, to declare what God has to say and not your aches and pains. The tongue can create good or bad in your life; that's why I say it is up to you to persistently work on making your tongue do what it was created to do; to produce life, to bless God the Father and the people around you. That's why Jesus said: "Bless and curse not," therefore, your tongue must do the duty it was created to do in order for you to move into your destiny.

When God created anything, he spoke the word; he said: "Let there be light" and there was light (Genesis 1:3). We are like God and have the same power to speak what we desire to see happen and when it comes to holding on to our healing this is very important.

You will never stay well if your confession is not in line with what the word of God is saying about your body. The more health you talk the more health you will have. That's why it's crucial that you must talk the talk of healing; not one day, but every day of your life.

CHAPTER 9

Walk the Walk

"Be ye doers of the word and not hearers only, deceiving your own selves."

"Be ye doers of the word and not hearers only deceiving your own selves" (James 1:22). Most of us who are born again Christians know this scripture by heart, but we don't always do it; in order to receive what God has promised in His word we must "WALK THE WALK," this is of course easier said than done and is not just a notion when pain is trying to persuade you to the other side of feeling and not believing. There is a fight or internal struggle that takes place.

Your feelings as I have stated in the previous chapters have nothing to do with your blood bought right as a born-again believer, as a matter a fact, as soon as you receive your healing you may not feel any differently, but that still does not mean you are not healed. It just means that your body has not yet caught up with your believing as of yet. If you continue to walk in the words that are spirit and life, your feelings, which is one aspect of your five physical senses will comply. It has no choice, because the heart which holds the word of God is greater than the natural man; the natural man must submit.

When I talk about walking the walk, of course I am talking about acting on His word. You must act on what you believe. You can't say one thing and do another; that is a contradiction of your faith. When we say one thing and do another our heart becomes confused and does not know what to bring forth. Your very existence is in your heart, when your mind is telling you "I can't" your faith should say "I can" and you should move forward in that vein.

I must be willing to obey and go in and possess the land that God has given me. In the Book of Numbers, ten (10) of the spies were not persuaded to enter into the Promised Land that God promised Abraham for the nations that would come forth from his son Isaac because of fear of what they saw and their own thinking. This is what happens when fear eclipses faith; it makes the promises of God null and void and causes God's people to unwillingly walk toward their destiny that God has promised them, although it's right in front of them. You must walk toward your destiny, not just seeing it and analyzing it will do you no good; you must move in the direction of what is in front of you; the Israelites weren't willing to move forward.

We talk a lot about the giants the spies saw, perhaps they were not giants at all. Perhaps the giants were figments of their minds. Sometimes the giants that we see in our lives paralyze us with fear and keep us from moving forward like the spies. We must be willing to move and possess the land that God has given each one of us, life is progressive, not static. After believing you must be willing to move forward not backward. You must have a vision for the future, if you don't you will not move forward.

I said walking was more than a notion and it is you have to believe God to the point that you will walk out on whatever He says for you to do. You must continue to feed your faith in order to keep walking. More importantly, you must feed your spirit man daily, when you feel like it and when you don't; if you feed your faith it will hold you in good stead when you need it most.

We must act out our faith. Why, because faith is an action word you can see faith at work. It always calls us to action. Whenever I stepped out in my faith, feeling always followed: "For as the body without the spirit is dead, so faith without works is dead also." (James 2:26) You don't always feel like moving out in your faith, but I can guarantee you when you do, your body will do its job and follow suit. Faith is a motivator, it keeps us walking the walk; we have been commanded to move forward so walking is a part of our destiny. When the commander and Chief tells us to act on the word of God that is exactly what we need to do.

Your confession is very important to your salvation. Allow your tongue to do its work. You will go no higher in your walk with God than your confession. You must confess something about your healing that was done at Calvary every single day. The word of God declares that Jesus is the High Priest of our confession. What I confess I possess. The first confession you should make out of your mouth is Jesus is Lord; if He is not Lord of all He is not Lord at all. In order for Him to be Lord over your body He must be Lord over your life. He has sworn to take care of what belongs to Him; we are not just his creation, "A new creature," we are his Body and He is the head of the Body and His body is not sick.

This should be one of your powerful consistent confessions; you are placed in the Earth to do a job for the KING. The only way He can complete what He has started is through your continual confession of His Lordship every single day.

CHAPTER 10

The Children's Bread

"For God so loved the world, that he gave his only begotten Son, the whoever believes in Him should not perish, but have everlasting life."

"Jesus said it was not right to take the children's bread and give it to dogs." (Matthew 15:26). What kind of statement was that? Was it just offensive or was it a true statement? It was both, but it brought healing to the woman's daughter. In order to receive the children's bread, she had to be willing to cross barriers she was unaccustomed to crossing. She had to be willing to take risks. She was not just a woman, but a Syrophoenician woman: a woman outside of the covenant of God at that time.

Like the Syrophoenician woman, you have to be desperate and desperately seeking what God has for you; especially when you know it belongs to you. As far as Jesus was concerned, this woman was not entitled to healing; but she was not going to let that stop her. Her daughter was demon possessed and she needed help. We need to understand that sickness in the body is demonic activity and when it presents itself to the body, it comes to possess it, yes, a body that does not belong to it, and the thing about demonic activity is that it does not always show up on x-rays because there is natural and there is spiritual.

Remember, we do not wrestle against flesh and blood, but against principalities and powers the rulers of the darkness of this world. In some kind of way, we must become like the Syrophoenician woman and not take no for an answer.

Satan likes to draw you into a long and hard battle when it comes to your health hoping you will give up and throw in the towel, but you must not because it is written "By whose stripes ye were healed" (1 Peter 2:24); that is past tense, that means it has already been done for you. This woman did not have that privilege, but she did not give up; she had such great faith, she made a demand on the promise and pulled it out of Him.

All we have to do today is walk in it and take it; we don't even have to ask, "It is the "Children's Bread." It is understood that it belongs to the children (the people of God). As a matter fact, he is rich towards all those who take it.

I have seen so many of God's Children die early when they did not have to. They had not lived their allotted time out in the Earth. The Book of Genesis declares that flesh can live 120 years: "Then the Lord said, My spirit will not contend with man forever, for they are mortal; their days will be a hundred and twenty years" (Genesis 6:3, NIV).

We have settled for less than and the people of God are dying at 70 and 80 years of age and some sooner. I know you think that is good but that is not the Church's promise; we need to reach one hundred twenty years (120) since that is God's will for us. Why not, if we are standing in faith for everything else, we need to start standing and believing for that so God can get the glory out of our lives.

This woman was not covenant but she believed God was gracious and merciful. We need to at least believe He is good to all those that trust in Him. God does not need us in heaven right away, He needs us here on planet Earth to demonstrate the devil's defeat. How do we do that? We do that by staying healed in our bodies so we can continue, like Paul, who said: "I have kept the faith, I have finished my course, and now I am ready to be offered up" (2 Timothy 4:7-8).

It's our bread, it's our sufficiency; it fills our lives with material, physical, and spiritual blessings, this is what God has promised His children and even the world. "God so loved the world that He gave his only begotten son, that whosoever would believe in him should not perish but have eternal life" (St. John 3:16).

This bread is the children's food; it's primarily what the children need. This woman knew that even the crumbs that fell from the table would be sufficient; she knew how powerful this bread was to even just desire the crumbs. We as believers and people don't have to settle, we can have the whole loaf. Why not take what rightfully belongs to us; when something rightfully belongs to you, why stand by and not take advantage of it.

CHAPTER 11

Some Reasons People Fail To Be Healed

"How God anointed Jesus of Nazareth with the Holy Spirit and power, who went about doing good and healing all who were oppressed by the devil, for God was with Him."

I often look at the following statement as very personal, but yet it needs to be stated and addressed: "How God anointed Jesus of Nazareth with the Holy Spirit and power, who went; about doing good and healing all that was Sick and oppressed of the devil. For God was with Him" (Acts 10:38 KJV).

My question is: "are we supposed to receive healing at all times?" Yes, this is the will of God concerning you, don't allow anyone to tell you anything different. The word of God does not change at any time and you believe Him for any and all things perpetually available for you to do a transaction with your faith, and because the word never changes it will always work on your behalf; why do some fail to get healed and others don't, I can only say what the word says: "All the promises of God are yes and amen to the glory of God the Father" (2 Corinthians 1:20); and the Father has said YES to your healing in your soul, body, and spirit. "Whose report do you believe?"

Walk out on and stand on the promises of God you will see glorious results. No one should fail to be healed; God is willing and wants you to have all he destined for you to have. Your future is a glorious unfolding and you can't allow sickness or disease to stop you.

WHAT SEEMS TO STOP SOME PEOPLE FROM GETTING THEIR HEALING?

1. THEY DON'T BELIEVE HEALING IS THEIR BLOOD BOUGHT COVENANT RIGHT: Healing belongs to us just as much as healing for the soul does. Some fail to see this as the same thing; you are just as much healed in your body as you are in your soul and spirit. Why, because they have become one. "I wish above all things that you would prosper and be in health even as your soul prospers" (3 John 1:2); the body soul and spirit should be in balance; that is the will of the Father.

2. FAILURE TO BELIEVE THE POWER OF THE CROSS: The cross as we talked about previously is a powerful tool when it comes to healing, even before Jesus went to the cross His body was beaten, battered, and bruised for our healing and when He died on the

cross He said: "it is finished," what was finished, the healing not just for the church, but the whole world.

3. FEARFUL: The Bible declares that "God hath not given us the spirit of fear but of power, love, and a sound mind" (2 Timothy 1:7). Fear will keep you from believing what God has actually freely given to you, healing is a free gift from God; if something goes wrong in the body it has already been placed in the spirit realm. Fear will keep you from accessing what is yours and keep you from staying here to complete your assignment; Satan would love to take you out before your assignment is over. As we discussed early on, your mind is very important and must be kept sound.

4. BELIEVING A LIE INSTEAD OF THE TRUTH: It all goes back to what you believe. The word of God is our road map from earth to glory, it brought

us here and it will take us home; how do you want to go home, in style, or diseased and infirmed; it's your choice. You may ask, how will I ever die if I don't get sick and die, well" ask Paul, he said: "I have fought a good fight I have kept the faith and now I am READY to be offered." He said I AM READY. Sounds to me he lived to finish the work God gave him to do. Don't believe the devils' lies, he would love to take you off the scene and he has no right, you would have to give him lead way or permission.

5. SIN CONSCIOUS: Nothing will kill your faith quicker for healing than being sin conscious when you are to be RIGHTEOUSNESS CONSCIOUS. Satan will try and tell us everything we haven't done right or what we have done wrong, and because we have not renewed our minds with the word of God. We become deceived only to believe the lies of the devil.

Jesus took care of all of that at the cross. He put sin away by the sacrifice of Himself (Hebrews 9:20).

6. NOT REMEMBERING WHO WE TRULY ARE IN GOD: "WHO TOLD YOU, YOU WERE NAKED?" Who told you that you are sick, have you partaken of the tree I told you not to partake of, have you been listening to the wrong voice? "My sheep know my voice and a stranger they will not follow" (St. John 10:27), they will not hear the voice of a stranger; if it's not the voice of God it is not the voice

CHAPTER 12

Spiritual eating vs natural eating

"The human body is fearfully and wonderfully made"

When we eat natural food, it passes through the gastrointestinal tract; it mixes with digestive juices, causes large pieces of food to break down into smaller pieces, the body then absorbs these smaller nutrients through the wall of the small intestines through the blood stream, which delivers them to the rest of the body. This feeds the body and gives it strength to do the job it needs to on a daily basis.

It matters what we put in the body to fuel it and cause it to work correctly. The spiritual food goes through the same process in order for us to be energized in the spirit. It matters what kind of food you feed your spiritual man, it must survive on its own kind; faith in God feeds the spiritual man, that's why you must feed your spiritual man the word of God.

When the word of God is processed through my spiritual man it produces Faith and without faith we know we cannot please God. You must feed your spirit just like you do your natural body; you would not put anything in your natural body that would be detrimental to your health and body; you want to fuel it with fruits, vegetables, water and the things that are good for the body so it can work responsibly. This is the same premise with the spirit; in order for our spirit man to be strong and work responsibly we must continue to wash it by the water of the word daily.

If you don't spend time in the word of God you will began to feel lethargic and not functioning on the level you should spiritually.

You have to feed your spirit a steady diet of God's word so when trouble presents itself your faith is ready and up for the challenge. The human body is "fearfully and wonderfully made" (Psalms 139:14) and God expects us to do our part in taking good care of it. The word of God declares that His word is "health to our flesh and strength to our bones" (Proverbs 3:8), so as you can see, besides eating correctly, the word of God is a cure for both sides, naturally and spiritually. In other words, the Bible declares HIS WORD IS HEALTH; and is not just a cure for the Spirit but also the Body and that we should eat properly on both sides of the fence. Proverbs 23:2 (KJV) says: "Put a knife to your throat if you are given to gluttony."

I am not talking about the Law saying

if you don't do this or that you can destroy your own body, I am saying that the Grace of God has shown us a better way to infiltrate one with the other. The law teaches us to be aware of how the principal of sowing and reaping operates in the universe and not sow to the flesh corruption. Diet is important, but a steady diet of God's word is even more important. "WATCH WHAT YOU EAT SPIRITUALLY AND NATURALLY.

Writing this book has caused me to reevaluate my eating habits and to make some permanent necessary changes. That's how the Holy Spirit is; he reminds us even when we are helping others to first help ourselves.

CHAPTER 13

Personal Testimonies' of God's Healing Power

Sister Tiffany Jeffers, Esquire

It was the last semester of my senior year of college. I was 20 years old, conquering my Political Science studies, believing I was invincible. Despite a few random and unrelated symptoms, I seemed to be very healthy and was enjoying life immensely. Little did I know; those random and unrelated symptoms would lead to the life altering diagnosis of an incurable disease.

At the beginning of my sophomore year of college, I began to suffer from a persistent cough. It happened initially when I laughed, and it brought chest pain with it. Initially, its persistence bothered me more than the chest pain. I saw a pulmonary specialist and they cleared me of tuberculosis and determined that I had some minor spotting on my lungs that could be treated (not cured) with antibiotics. I added the antibiotics to my routine, but the cough worsened. There were days when the cough was uncontrollable and I would end up coughing up blood. On one occasion, I was admitted to the emergency room and subsequently released with no diagnosis and more antibiotics. Also, I began to lose significant amounts of weight; I attributed the weight loss to me shedding "baby fat" and was excited that my body was slimming down. I entered college weighing 168lbs and by my junior year, I was down to 130lbs. I can't lie...I loved it! I was ecstatic that for the first time in my life I was able to fit single digit sizes and it was happening in the prime of life!!

The most debilitating symptom that I experienced during this time was fatigue; fatigue is always a tricky symptom because you don't want to mistakenly label lack of sleep or a long day as fatigue, but this feeling of exhaustion was ever-present and no matter how much rest I got, I always felt tired. I thought it was just a consequence of pulling all-nighters to finish papers, study for exams, or attend a hot party. The breaking point came during my winter break in 2003.

I was home for Christmas and I had lost so much weight that my older sister thought I had an eating disorder. The cough worsened, and the chest pain became exacerbated just by breathing. I developed a swollen lymph node on my neck and my parents demanded that I go to the emergency room. The attending physician in the emergency room was calming and reassured my family that I was young and healthy and was likely suffering from a virus. We were told that swollen lymph nodes were a symptom of infection and that I definitely shouldn't worry because the node wasn't cancer.

I went back to school to begin my final semester prior to graduation; my friends noticed that the lump on my neck seemed to be growing and encouraged me to go to health services on campus, I obliged. I saw the nurse practitioner on campus and she measured the node. She seemed more concerned than the ER physician back home, which piqued my interest; she referred me to an Ear, Nose and Throat (ENT) specialist to have a biopsy completed. I went to the ENT appointment and had the biopsy done and moved on with my life.

I remember receiving a call from the campus health services asking me if I could come to campus to discuss the results of my recent appointment. It still hadn't registered to me that something significant was taking place; my naivety kept me in a perpetual state of calmness. I went to campus and sat down in the Dean's office, the chief of campus health services, and Dean of Student Affairs were present; they asked if there was a family member that they could call on speaker phone. I told them to call my sister who was local because my parents and other sister were 2000 miles away. With my sister on speaker phone, I was told that the biopsy done on my swollen lymph node had come back with malignant cells and that I was being referred to an oncologist. The rest of the meeting is mostly a blur because although I was not pre-med, I had a working knowledge of the words "malignant" and "oncologist".

The diagnosis phase was quick. I made an appointment with the oncologist that I was referred to; she was a beautiful Black woman that seemed eager to jump in and work with my family and scheduled surgery to remove the lymph node and have it tested to confirm a diagnosis.

During the interim between the removal of the lymph node and diagnosis, I had several PET and CT scans. Finally, the day came where my oncologist gave me the diagnosis of Stage IV Hodgkin's Lymphoma. The cancer had spread throughout my body and was in my neck; my spleen; my left lung; and my groin. The cancer was aggressive, which meant that treatment had to be even more aggressive. My oncologist scheduled me to have chemotherapy once every three weeks for a period of seven months. I cried. I was in a state of relief and a state of shock. The relief was related to finally having an answer for the symptoms that I had been experiencing for the better part of two years; the shock came because the diagnosis was Stage IV Cancer...the Big C.

I began treatment with a renewed mind to beat cancer with the support of my family, friends and professors and a top notch medical team that guided my treatment. Most importantly, I had a supportive church family that regularly prayed for my healing. I had spoken to my classmates and made arrangements to write papers in lieu of class attendance. The faculty and college administration were supportive of my endeavor to graduate on time despite the aggressive treatment schedule. The treatments were difficult and left me feeling weak and sick.

It was interesting because I appeared to be getting healthier on the outside. My hair was full (even despite the awful haircut that I received in anticipation of losing my hair), my skin was glowing, and I actually looked fantastic... at first. There were good weeks and bad weeks, but I pressed on because I just knew that I would overcome this. I had placed a huge amount of faith and trust in my own ability to survive and the support and encouragement that I was receiving from friends and family.

I didn't realize that God was not using cancer as a method for me to believe in myself or my ability to do anything, but that it was a call to fully trust and rely on Him as the source of my strength, health and overall existence (this revelation would come later). There were moments where I wanted to quit, but I would get an encouraging word from a friend and I would continue on. I graduated with my class and even secured a full-time job at a law firm. Life was good, and because life was good, I thought God was good. I finished my seven months of treatment and was permitted one month free of doctor's appointments before my oncologist required updated scans.

Basically, after the seven months of treatment, I received a tentative all clear from my physician. I was very optimistic that when I came back for the updated scans I would be cancer free. I honestly do not remember the appointment for the follow up scans, but I remember receiving a call from my oncologist on my 22nd birthday; she called to inform me that the cancer had returned in a more aggressive form.

I went to her office and she explained that I had received the most potent chemotherapy drugs for that treatment regimen and the only available next step was a stem cell transplant. I sat in her office alone and in disbelief. I felt numb, powerless, and angry at God for what I thought was the false hope of healing. I remember telling my oncologist that I did not want a stem cell transplant, I did not want any more chemotherapy and that I was going to change my diet and go all natural. My oncologist looked me in my eyes and told me that if I did not have this treatment, I would die.

I left that appointment devastated. It was my birthday and I had just received a second cancer diagnosis. I went to the chapel in the hospital and prayed;

actually, I just sat on the pew. I asked God why this was happening again just when it seemed like things were finally going right for me. I stayed in the chapel alone for an hour or so and then I called my sister and my best friend to pick me up from the hospital. They took me to dinner and I tried my best to process the information I had just received.

I had to go to work and tell my manager that my cancer had returned and that I would need to take a leave of absence. Looking back, I am extremely grateful at how accommodating my employer was. I had only been with the law firm for three months when I was re-diagnosed.

The diagnosis and staging process moved quickly; just as it had the first time. The difference was that my supportive group was not close at hand to cheer me on. All of my friends from college had moved away and started jobs in different cities. My family had returned home and the excitement of beating cancer that was present when I was diagnosed the first time had faded. This was a very dark time in my life. I vividly remember trying to be optimistic while explaining to the new oncology team that I had not lost my hair with the first round of treatment. They were kind, but firm in their explanation that this transplant utilized the most potent form of chemotherapy to date. The drugs were created to totally eradicate my entire immune system in the hopes of killing every cancer cell. Not only did they tell me that I would lose my hair, they told me that this treatment would make me weak and very sick and because I would have no immune system, I would be unable to live with my sister as I had been doing; I would have to move into a sterilized environment and when in public, I would have to wear a mask.

This was so different than the lively chemo sessions where friends and family visited for hours while I received treatment. I had to be isolated and the enemy knew that isolating me was the first step to waging war against my mind.

Prior to beginning treatment, I planned one last public outing with some friends and family. We went to dinner and to see the movie "The Passion of the Christ." I was so inspired by the movie that I chose that day to use my isolation period to devote my life totally to Christ. I decided in the movie theatre that if Jesus could suffer the Cross for my sins, then I could endure the modern medicine designed to simultaneously kill and heal my body.

Once I made that decision, things got worse. Physically, I was tolerating treatment. I lost my hair and I was weak, but the enemy began to come against me in a way that I had never experienced before. One night as I was sleeping, I felt a dark presence in my bedroom and then suddenly I was unable to move or speak. In my mind I was screaming, but it felt like something was holding me down and had taken away the sound from my mouth; I remember thinking the words, "the Blood of Jesus" and everything immediately ceased, the evil dissipated from the room and I regained possession of my faculties.

Another time, I fell into a dark depression and the enemy began speaking directly to me. Satan told me that if I chose to serve him, that he could heal me, also, he told me that I was already created in his image because I resembled the character that played Satan in the movie "The Passion of the Christ." I remember that I did not verbally respond to the words of the enemy, but in my heart, I was determined to follow Jesus and I simply said NO. I was never again approached by demonic spirits in those same overt manners, but the attack for my joy and faith remained. I knew that the only way to strengthen my faith and encourage myself was to begin to spend time with Jesus through the Holy Spirit. I began reading God's Word and praying regularly. I wrote in my journal daily about the goodness of God even though I was sick and weak from my treatment.

I began to understand that God was going to use my situation for His glory. I continued with my treatment regimen. I received a stem cell transplant four months after my re-diagnosis. My stem cell transplant was successful and in addition to physical healing, I received a healing of my mind and spirit. I learned that healing requires faith and the most efficient and effective way to build our faith is to spend time with God's Word.

I felt the most complete during and immediately after because I was open to receive what God had for me. It was during the lowest point in my life that I realized that God merely wanted my commitment. The Holy Spirit yearns to give us revelation, but often times we are too busy to hear. I am thankful that God created a space and season for me to be in complete and total reliance on Him.

The true healing came not through medicine, but through being relational with God the Father, God the Son and God the Holy Spirit.

Sister Jeanie Stanfield

My name is Jeanie Stanfield and I was diagnosed with Thyroid Cancer on April 4th, 2013. Prior to that I had experienced symptoms that were new to me, but when I went to the hospital the last thing I expected was the diagnosis that I had a big tumor pressing against my wind pipe. When the doctor examined me, he said I needed surgery right away. I also had another problem; I did not have any medical insurance. However, my case was so dire the doctor said he would waive the insurance requirement.

In other words, if I did not have surgery I would die.

I had surgery on Thursday, July 25, 2013, and the doctors had their doubts about my chances to survive. Immediately after the procedure to remove the tumor, they had to go back in my throat because I had a blood clot. Following that, the doctor told my mom to get my affairs in order.

I was hooked up to several machines to keep me alive, but I heard God say it was not my time to die. I had people praying for me and I know God heard their prayers. I was in the hospital eleven (11) days and during that time I lay there giving God the praise. When I left the hospital, I went to church with my mom. At the time, I was not a regular churchgoer, but when I left the hospital I made a commitment to go; I became very active in Church.

From that time on, I could be found in church thanking and praising the Lord for deliverance because I know if it had not been for the Lord I wouldn't be alive; and when I awake, when I eat, when I go to bed at night I say "THANK YOU LORD!!" He has been incredibly good to me and I know I'm blessed.

Even now, my journey and testimony is not finished. After my procedure, the doctor put a feeding tube in me, but the tube did not work well with my system. As a result, the doctor decided to take my feeding tube out prematurely. Most people would be alarmed, but this was just another chance for God to show His glory. I started eating on my own after that and I have been eating on my own ever since.

After all this, I still was not out of the woods. Later, I had to have radiation therapy and as a result of the radiation, I lost all of my teeth; but I endured, survived, and I came through the radiation fine just loosing teeth, but, through the glory of God I was able to get Four thousand dollars' worth of dentures!

On July 7, 2016, I had another operation to remove the rest of my lymph nodes. They had not gotten them out during my first operation because they were too small, but by now they had gotten large enough to be removed. It was scary because they had to operate very close to the veins in my neck. Once again, the Lord came through for me and I came out healthy. Through all my trials with cancer I just keep praising and thanking God and he keeps delivering me.

Each and every day I take time to say thank you God for healing and saving me. The doctor's believed that I would not make it even as they were operating on me, but by God I am alive to bear witness! I still have to go to the hospital every six (6) months to get a CT scan and a MRI; each time I go I see the hand of God at work in my life. I am healthy, cancer free and continually say: "thank you Lord for saving, healing, and changing my life for the better."

Deacon Christopher Hinton

My name is Christopher (Chris) Hinton and this is my testimony of God's deliverance. I was a drinker and a drug user for many years. I started drinking when I was a senior in high school. I went into the military and got stationed in Germany for two and a half years. When I got there, I hit it off with my roommates immediately. The guys I roomed with were from different States. We got into drinking a lot of liquor and smoking dope pretty soon after we met. We thought it was helping us loosen up and we did have a lot of fun laughing and telling jokes. After a while the marijuana and drinking was not a good enough high anymore for us, so we started smoking a stronger form of weed called "hash" and snorting cocaine. When I left Germany, and came home I brought my drug and drinking habit with me. I came home and eventually married my high school sweetheart Tammy. While I was away she had gotten saved, but I still kept on drinking and doing drugs; through it all, I kept a job.

I knew I hit rock bottom when one payday I received the biggest paycheck I had ever gotten. I should have taken that check home to my wife and paid my bills, but instead I spent it all going from crack house to crack house. When I finally came down from my all-night crack runs, I felt horrible. I knew I was a disappointment to my family and I was disappointed in myself.

I got so low I began contemplating suicide. I decided instead to go home and face the consequences. Predictably when I got home my wife was rightfully furious and going to leave me but her sister who is a minister came over and told her that I needed her more than ever during this dark time.

To her credit, my wife did not leave me because love is powerful, and it endures and always sees the best in you even when you aren't being the best. Instead, she invited me to church. When I got to church the Pastor was preaching and it seemed he knew my life. I got up at the altar call and accepted Jesus Christ as my lord and savior. Instead of hanging around on the street, I started hanging around the elders in the church. I began going to Sunday school and bible study to learn about Jesus Christ, how He died for my sins, and how He desperately wants a relationship with me. Through God's grace and glory, I am now a Deacon in church and I am fully delivered and healed of my addiction.

I share this testimony because I want anyone who is suffering from the disease of addiction to know that Jesus can heal and deliver you also.

Sister Karen Evans

It all started in 2014, around November, when I was diagnosed with hyper-thyroidism. Thyroid problems can come on suddenly and initially I didn't have too many health issues. However, 2015, I lost a lot of weight and also lost my appetite for about three (3) weeks. I then went to the E.R. and they said I needed surgery because they thought my gall bladder was enlarged. As they prepped me for surgery, I began to pray. As I prayed, I called my sister who called other prayer partners for support. Miraculously, the doctors came the next morning and said I didn't need surgery. Immediately my appetite was restored, and the doctors said I could be on a regular diet, they then brought me a menu and I ordered food.

I still had some issues from my thyroid problem; I had a rapid heartbeat and I also had some damage to my liver; the doctors gave me medication for those issues. Thanks to God my liver started improving and my heart rate returned to normal within a matter of days.

I credit my healing to prayer, prayer changes your situation all around, the prayers of the righteous avails much; within four days I was able to go home. Once I was home I started seeing a endocrinologist. He prescribed me some medicine, but he also said everything was looking a lot better. I began to eat better and gain weight; within a few months I was able to return to my normal life.

Later I started having problems with my stomach. I went to the doctor and they said they could not find anything. I lost my appetite and couldn't keep any food down. Even though I was in pain I tried to stick to my regular routine.

About 4 days later I went to work, but my stomach hurt so badly I had to leave. That night I was sitting watching T.V. and I heard something pop. I had the worst pain in my stomach. I couldn't stand up and I knew I needed to call 911. I wasn't near my phone and my roommate was upstairs. All I could do was crawl on the floor until I reached a wall. I just knocked on the wall until my roommate came downstairs to see what was going on. What

she discovered was me on the floor in the fetal position, she asked what was wrong with me, and I let her know what was happening, she immediately called 911 and waited with me until the ambulance arrived. They came in and rushed me to the ER. Tests revealed that I had a burst ulcer; the doctors said I needed surgery right away.

I remember getting ready for surgery; the nurse came in and said they were going to give me something to slow my heart; before they put me under I called my son and sisters to let them know what was happening. When I woke up my family was all around me. I could remember who everyone was, but I really didn't know if it was night or day because there were no windows in ICU. Wherever I looked there were all kinds of tubes, I had a tube in my neck, arms, nose, mouth, feet, stomach and around my head. I wasn't aware of what had happened to me. The Dr. came in and reminded me that I had surgery to remove a burst ulcer. I couldn't walk, talk, or breathe on my own; and I was hooked up to a heart monitor. It felt like my heart was beating 160 miles a second and I had staples in my stomach; on top of all that, my thyroid was out of control. My sugar levels where up, my blood pressure was very high and my potassium levels were low. I had IVs in both arms and I had a catheter because I couldn't use the bathroom on my own.

Everything in my body had basically shut down; later my son told me, "mom you died and came back in the room."

I actually went into cardiac arrest during the operation, but I pulled through. The ulcer condition was actually caused by my thyroid problem; at that point I knew all I could do was rely on God. I asked my son to play praise and worship music. I prayed and asked God to heal my body. I distinctly heard God say, "I'm going to take care of you." From that moment on, my situation began to change. Eventually, they took the tube out of my mouth. I slowly started eating again, liquids first and then they came and took the tubes out of my neck. Next, I was able to move out of ICU to another room. Soon I was able to get up with help. My son was there, and he was a huge help.

I have to say God is amazing and always keeps his promise. I took pleasure in little victories; I was able to bathe myself and I started walking with a walker. I got stronger and stronger each day. After a while, I started dressing myself. Then the doctors took the catheter out. The doctors were amazed at my progress, they said if everything kept going the way it was going they would let me go home very soon.

They finally stopped pricking my fingers and my heart rate began to line up with the word of God. In a short time, they took all the IVs out and they took out the tube in my nose. One day an occupational therapist came to see me; she couldn't believe how well I had recovered and called me her Christmas miracle (my hospitalization happened in mid-December.). When I got home, with God's help, I continued to progress. Every day I felt stronger and could do more things for myself.

Today I am healed, delivered, and made whole. I don't need a walker or a heart monitor. God had strengthened me and I'm back at church and work. I have a work out regiment and I'm back to living life to the fullest. God is faithful to his children. As I prayed and got closer with God, he brought to my remembrance some of the things I saw while sedated.

The feeling I have is like I got a chance to see heaven. I remember being in the sky with smooth skin; the air was clear, and I could see more clearly than I ever had. Other people were there too,and I knew it was not their physical bodies I was seeing but their spirits. We all looked unbelievable. It was like we were getting ready to put on a show. I know that's how paradise will be. Praise God!

Sister Yvonne Harrington

It all began in January of 1989. I cannot quite remember the exact day and time but I know it was at night. While I was sitting on my sofa holding my 3-year-old daughter, I started experiencing what felt like a fever along with pains in my stomach. I just had a general feeling of disease in my whole body. No matter how hard I tried, I could not ignore the pains and I was in chronic discomfort throughout the night. I thought it would go away the next day, but the pains just got increasingly worse. Out of concern I called my mother. I told her how I was feeling and that I needed her to go with me to my doctor's office. I was worried and wanted to have an evaluation done because I felt like the pain I was experiencing was out of the ordinary.

When we got to the clinic, the nurse asked me to describe my symptoms. They told me they needed to draw some blood and run some tests to identify the source of my illness. Afterwards, my mother and I were told to wait for the results.

After a few minutes the results were back, and it wasn't good news. I was definitely not prepared for what they had to say. They diagnosed me with LEUKEMIA. I was confused; neither my mother nor I had a full understanding of what the diagnosis meant. They told us to go directly to Norfolk General Hospital because my condition was very serious, and I needed immediate medical attention. My mother became very upset and wanted to gain a clear understanding of the disease. When she asked the medical staff about Leukemia, the answer made it more realistic, tangible and plainly understood. I was told that I had blood cancer and it was very advanced.

With a new sense of understanding about the urgency of my situation, we wasted no time getting to the hospital. After we arrived at the hospital and completed the admissions paperwork I was quickly assigned to a regular hospital room. They immediately began administering aggressive Chemotherapy.

Things were happening so fast and I don't really remember much about what was going on, however, I do remember the loss of appetite, the inability to keep anything down, the inability to walk without support, and the drastic weight loss; my weight dropped from 130 pounds to 78 pounds and I could feel my energy being sapped. Although they were doing their best to treat the cancer, my condition worsened. Eventually, I developed pneumonia which precipitated my move to the ICU.

Just as I was about to be moved into ICU, my daughter-in-law and her mother came to visit me, and I praise the Lord that they did; I was afraid because I had not accepted Jesus as my personal Savior.

Lying there in my condition allowed me time to contemplate what would happen to my soul if I were to not make it through. My daughter-in-law as well as her mother took the time to minister to me; they told me all about the Gospel of Jesus Christ; how much He loved me, died for my sins, and could heal me of ALL my diseases. They prayed with me and with a sincere heart, I accepted Jesus Christ as my personal Savior and repented of my sins.

Once I was situated in the ICU room, I remember that they hooked me up to a heart monitor and other medical equipment, but my condition continued to deteriorate. Due to the pneumonia, I had difficulty breathing on my own, my lungs were filling up with fluid and they began to collapse. The doctor explained to me that I had to be intubated. This meant he would have to place an endotracheal tube down my throat and hook me up to an oxygen machine.

As time progressed and my treatment continued, I remember the day my family came into the ICU to visit with me. What was unusual about it is my whole family was there and they came in the room one by one. As I lay there I began wondering why they were all there to see me at the same time. What I didn't know was that my family was called by the medical staff and told that I had less than a 10% chance of surviving the weekend, albeit, the medical staff was working according to their medical training and experience. According to their guidelines my prognosis wasn't good and that necessitated them to notify my family so that they could prepare and plan for my funeral; but God had a different plan.

Fortunately, I had given my life to Christ and I sent my prayers up. My daughter-in-law did her part by not letting any negative energy enter my situation; she told the medical staff not to let me know my prognosis and I did my part by fighting the battle and not giving up. I kept the faith and believed that The Lord Jesus Christ was going to bring me through. As the days passed, my heart got stronger and I began breathing on my own. Eventually, the doctor came in and removed the tube from my throat and I was moved from ICU to a regular room.

After I got settled in my room, a nurse came in to check my vital signs. Standing at the foot of my bed she said, "Ms. Harrington, you SHOULD be dead. You had less than a 10% chance of living this past weekend."

That's the healing power of the God that I serve! Satan thought he had me. However, I knew that I had Jesus on my side and Satan could not change my way of thinking. Satan was so angry that he told me to jump out of the window that was next to my bed because I was not getting better. I could not talk back to him because I had that breathing tube down my throat, but I still had a good clear mind to let him know my answer was "NO!" My God said that He would get me out of here ALIVE and made whole."

A few days later, my doctor came in and with a smile, asked: "Are you ready to go home?" With tears falling down my face, I nodded my head yes. He stated, "You will be going home tomorrow. You are a MIRACLE and I will write this in your folder." It's just that I had the Lord Jesus Christ on my side and in the Word it says... "But He was wounded for our transgressions, He was bruised for our iniquities, the chastisement of our peace was upon Him; and with His stripes we are healed." (Isaiah 53:5).

This is my testimony to those that have doubt and believe there is no God. I am telling you from my personal experience, I would not be alive today if it had not been for the love of Jesus. Jesus saves and loves you too. Please accept Him today as your personal Savior.

CHAPTER 14

Having Done All Stand

"Let us hold fast to the profession of our faith without wavering."

Learning how to stand on the word of God for healing is more than a notion. It not only takes faith it takes guts, your adversary the devil walks around seeking who will fall for his lies. The moment you have made a resolution to stand on God's word for healing he is there to move you off your stance. You have to be fully persuaded just like Abraham and not stagger or waver one bit on the promise of God. Your mind must be made up and your heart fixed that this is it; I will not relent, but will rely on God fully for the results in my body.

The word of God has spoken and that settles every issue of the problem that has come up against you. Let's talk about Abraham; the Bible declares he did not stagger at the promise of God, but considered his own body to be dead. He knew his flesh would be no help to him at all. That was the thing he was up against. He could not consider what his body was telling him, instead he concentrated on the one who had promised him victory; he did not even look to Sarah for help, because he knew she could do no more than he could. She was flesh and blood just like him, and as far as man was concerned, they were in the same place as he was. Abraham did not consider his wife being able to give him a little hope, that's why the bible talked about hope against hope, speaking naturally; there was nothing for Abraham to look to other than God.

I think sometimes when we are in a trying place; God will allow anything that would give us hope in the natural to be removed. I did not say God brought sickness into the world, upon his people because I don't believe God would try and teach his children lessons through sickness and disease; that's the devil's territory. As I stated before, sickness and disease does not come from a loving heavenly Father; sickness is death operating in the body and God is not the author or finisher of death. He is the author and finisher of our faith.

"Yes! All power in heaven and earth belongs to him, but God chose to give the earth to the children of men and what they choose in this realm is theirs. Sickness and disease does not have dominion over you, you have dominion over it. "All things are yours" (1 Corinthians 3:21). God chose Abraham, but Abraham also chose God; the Bible states that "Abraham believed God." When you believe God, you have chosen Him and you will have the same opportunity as Abraham did to stand without wavering; instead, Abraham was strengthened in his faith, giving God glory.

As believer's, we will always have the opportunity to stand on one thing or another; however, I don't like to say you will have to stand against the spirit of infirmity, but that's one of those giants who will try and stand on your land and you will have the opportunity to tell him where to take it because you are not giving him not one inch of your territory; that's why standing is so imperative. When someone comes and tries to take something from you that is rightfully yours you will not stand by and do nothing; you will not let anyone take what is rightfully yours, by birth right, "WHAT'S YOURS IS YOURS" and you are not going to allow anyone to take dominion of what has been given to you by birth.

Healing is your inheritance; it belongs to you, it's your rite of passage. No, no, no a thousand times no, fight the good fight of faith, lay hold to your right to walk in Divine health like a honey badger holds on to its prey and if you get knocked down, shake yourself and get up for the next round until your faith comes to manifestation.

Healing Is Yours, Stand on God's Word, He Is Faithful Who Promised.

CHAPTER 15

Defying The Urge To Quit

"I always triumph in Christ"

You must never give up on your manifestation for healing; the scripture declares "we were healed," that is past tense, so for you to give in and stop standing on the word would be utter foolishness; God has given us his word and that is our faith. We must defy anything that gives us the urge to quit. Paul declared: "I always triumph in Christ" (2 Corinthians 2:14).

We must continue to believe and stand in faith until we see the tide turn in our favor. The enemy will put pressure on your body to get you to give in and declare with your mouth the wrong thing, and as you know, whoever has the gateway to the mouth and the mind, to the victor goes the spoils.

Satan loves to apply pressure to get you to question the validity of God's word, but if you will stay focused on what God said and be a doer of the word you will win every time. God has made you a promise about your body and he will keep that promise if you will remind yourself every day that "By whose stripes we were healed" (1 Peter 2:24) which puts the word of God in past tense, which means it has already been done. So, the last thing you should even consider is quitting.

Know there is someone out there right now, even as you read this book who's thinking about quitting, don't you do it, stay in the race and move to the next level. YOU CAN MAKE IT! Keep pressing and believing the victory has already been won. Your

body will respond the way your spirit responds. The spirit of a man will sustain his infirmity; but a wounded spirit who can bear (Proverbs 18:14 KJV)? When you feel like giving up you are missing out on Gods best; God has promised to be with you whereever you go; what if we quit when we are right at the door. We will miss the mark. How many people have given up when the answer was so close, "let us hold fast our confidence until the end" (Hebrews 3:6 NASB); God is faithful to do what he said he would do. Remember, the spirit world is more real than the natural world. We look not at the things that are seen it is the things we do not see with the natural eye that are more real and better. Some people would say: "seeing is believing;" but in the spiritual world God has called us to "believing is seeing;" the whole of heaven is backing you up, trust and never doubt; He will surely bring you out; defy the urge to quit and God will show you his word is true.

To the Victor Goes the Spoils.

CHAPTER 16

The Heart Will Keep the Body

"And the very God of peace sanctify you wholly; and I pray God your whole spirit, soul, and body be preserved blameless unto the coming of our Lord Jesus Christ."

1 THESSALONIANS 5:23

Man is three dimensional, he is made up of spirit, soul, and body, his soul is made up of his mind, will, and emotions; our body, which is the temple or home of the spirit. Your spirit is the real you. This is where things are carried out for your life. The Bible tells us to guard the heart because out of it flow the issues of life; our life is in our heart this is why you must guard it. "If any man be in Christ he is a new creature old things are passed away behold all things have become new" (2 Corinthians 5:17) and because we are new creatures we have to think new and allow new things to be deposited in our heart; we cannot allow anything that's not like God in our spirit man. When trouble comes, our heart must know what to produce. We must not allow our hearts to be confused with evil.

When we were born again God recreated our spirit in His righteousness. We are the righteousness of God in Christ Jesus. Therefore, we are who God says that we are and we can do what God says we can do; we have the ability to guard our hearts, we don't have to let anything in our heart that doesn't give life. If we don't protect our heart our body will not be protected either; so, goes the heart so goes the body. The heart runs the body that's why we are in charge of our heart to make sure nothing goes in there that's not supposed to be there. Your mind and your body were not made new, but your spirit was. "But let it be the hidden man of the heart, in that which is not corruptible even the ornament of a meek and quiet spirit, which is in the sight of God of great price" (1 Peter 3:4). Your spirit needs to stay clean because the issues of life flow out of it, this means what you have on the inside can sustain you when you are sick.

When Satan attacks the body of a believer, the Spirit of the Lord immediately lifts up a standard against the enemy recognizing that there is an unauthorized foul alien attempting to not only attack but supernaturally attach itself to the believer and try to kill, steal, or destroy the believer. Please note, the believer(s) whose inner man or spirit has been fortified with the Word of God will wage a spiritual battle against this alien force of darkness and triumph victoriously because they are aware of the fact that: "the weapons of our warfare are not carnal but mighty through God to the pulling down of strong holds (2 Corinthians 10:4)", that's why it is very important to guard the heart.

The body is the clothing for the spirit and it is so important for our bodies to be in good health or healthy in order for us to do the will of God on the Earth. Our heart is the ground in which the seed of the word is deposited; therefore, the soil of our hearts must be good ground. What I mean by that is we must make sure that what we allow in our hearts will be conducive to helping the body to stay well. Envy, jealousy, and strife will not help the body stay well, it must be good ground, solid, fertile ground in order for the seed to produce what it needs to produce and in the time of trouble, disappointments, crises, hurt, disasters, and uncertainty, the seed of God's word will respond to the situation and produce what needs to be productive and fruitful in your life at that particular time. Therefore, we must take time to study all that God says in His word about healing; the seed works mightily in me and will do the same for you.

Jesus talked about the "sower" who sows the word. We are responsible for sowing the word in our heart on a daily basis; when we do this, Satan does not have a chance to sow his evil in us. How do we "sow", by diligently studying the word of God and listening to what God has to say about our healing.

Once the word of God is deposited in your heart, you must not let Satan steal the word of God out of your heart. Jesus tells us to hold fast to what we have because He knew the enemy of our soul and soil would come to steal the word that had been sown.

Also, the pressures of life come to steal the word out of your heart so you can become unfruitful. It is your job to hold fast the word in your heart. When you learn how to stand and hold the word fast, it won't be as easy for the enemy to steal your healing or anything else that God has freely given you. Also, you must recognize and appreciate what has been freely given to you and make a demand on your heart when it comes times to produce the fruit thereof.

Your heart will know what to believe when you have deposited the truth and it will come to your remembrance when you need it most. Again, your heart is the most important organ in your body, protect it at all cost; make sure the right things enter in your heart so that your body will respond favorably.

Satan will come to snatch the word out of your heart if you let him; unbelief, persecution, and tradition of men will make the word of God of no effect. Tradition will tell you God is no longer healing; but that is not true, it is written in God's word it cannot change. God has spoken.

CHAPTER 17

"Daughter Be of Good Comfort; Thy Faith That Made Thee Whole."

ST. MATTHEW 9:22

It is your faith that will make you whole; Jesus told the woman with the issue of blood it was her faith that had done the job. People often think it is God who makes us whole or who makes us believe Him, but God has done everything he is ever going to do for us when it comes to our Salvation. He hadn't even gone to the cross under the Abrahamic Covenant, but yet He told the woman "her faith had made her whole." As far as God was concerned, even from the beginning, sickness and disease had been dealt with and if this woman could believe, anything would be possible for her, even being healed.

It will be your faith that will make you whole because the work at the cross has already been dealt with. It is our job to take what is rightfully ours. We must not give in to the voice of unbelief, doubt, and reason. These three things will rob you of your blessing of walking in divine health every time.

The Bible declared the woman was made whole that very hour. Think about it, that very hour which means her faith went to work immediately, she could have had her healing long before if she had allowed her faith to work. Jesus said her FAITH, not Him. What you get from God now will be by faith. As a Christian, your faith is supposed to supply you with whatever you need in this life. The woman with the issue of blood felt she needed a point of contact, so she touched his garment, but the only point of contact we need is the word of God.

There was nothing wrong with what she did during that time because Jesus had not died and given us a right to the tree of life, but now it is different. The price has been paid and we must remember that we have been made whole through the blood of the Lamb. Jesus left nothing to chance, the full price was paid; we must now believe in the work that was done for our healing: "Believe ye that I am able to do this?" (Matthew 9:28).This was one of the questions Jesus asked before the manifestation of healing and after the cross: "Do you believe I have done this?" It must be in past tense, why, because at the cross it was finished.

The question could be asked under the Abrahamic Covenant, but certainly the question must not be in our minds as to whether or not Jesus did a complete work; to say "I believe He can do this" would question His validity as to whether He did it at all; we must be like Father Abraham, fully persuaded. At that time, they said "YEA LORD" which was a good answer; but our answer now should be "THANK YOU LORD!" I believe, I receive my healing, and thank you since it belongs to me!

CHAPTER 18

He Cast Out the Spirits With a Word, and Healed All Who Were Sick

"He cast out the spirits with a word, and healed all who were sick."

MATTHEW 8:16

We talked about words before, but they are so important when it comes to one living in healing or divine health. We must talk healing if we are to walk in it; just as Jesus cast out spirits with his words, so can we. We must make our mouth and actions agree with God's word in order for God's word to be fulfilled in our lives. The word of God is his divine power; we are to trust in His word and His word alone.

When a challenge comes against our body we must stand on the word and say what the word of God says about our healing. Challenges will always present themselves in life, we must hold on to the word of God in order to meet that challenge. There are many spirits that will be cast out with your words; you will heal with your words because your words are power packed and are very important.

Learn to speak words of "Health, Healing, and Wholeness." Your body will obey your words. Speaking the word over your body each day is a good way to remind yourself on a daily basis of what God said about your health and well-being and "By

whose stripes ye were healed;" reminding us of what has already been done for us and all we have to do is lay hold of it by faith.

Further, we must remember that the way we lay hold of it is through our words. Also, we cast out the spirit of sickness and disease with what we say and do; we must act on what has been done and said, this pertains not just to the children of God, but to everyone who will receive what the word of God has spoken.

The Bible declared that He healed all who were sick. Jesus did not leave anyone out; all who were standing, lying; or kneeling were healed. ALL MEANS ALL. Remember we discussed that in the Old Testament there was not one feeble one among them, it had to be God's will to heal all that were sick, and He did it with his word.

How are we going to walk in healing or divine health with His word in our mouth at all times? We cannot talk foolishness and stay healed or walk in divine health; why, because our tongue deceives our heart; the heart will not bring forth good things if we do not put good things in it; healing or divine health is a good thing; how do we deposit good things in our heart? David said: "my tongue is as the pen of a ready writer" (Psalm 45:1); "write these words upon the table of your heart" (Proverbs 7:3) by saying what God says.

Whatever you put in your heart is what will come out. When the pressures of life come, your heart will be ready to aid and help you through these pressures. Talk Gods word every single day, remind your heart of who you really are and when you need it; your heart will remind you. If I may remind you from the previous chapters, it's not God's will for anyone to be sick, He wants us well so that we may live a prosperous and fulfilling life for Him.

God wants the whole world to see how much He loves and honors his children by them staying healthy and whole; there is no greater testimony to the Lords goodness than for us to stay whole in our bodies, not just our soul and spirit. Our body is where the Holy Spirit dwells so we must protect this house and cast out unwanted spirits with HIS WORD. Satan is an opportunist; he will take advantage of any ground you give him. We are not to give him one inch of our land that the Lord has so freely given to us.

Yes, divine healing is part of that land. God wants us to understand that we are just as much healed as we are saved. The Church needs to be taught vigorously about healing just as much as their Salvation. We must keep the word of God in our mouth to stop Satan at every turn. "He cast out the spirit with His word and healed all who were sick," notice He did not leave anyone out. He healed all of them. In conclusion, let your mouth do its job and cast out every manner of sickness and disease.

21 Day Journal To Health, Healing, and Wholeness"

It is evident that God has healed and does have the power to heal our physical bodies.

Miraculous healings still happen today.

This 21 Day journal will aid you on the road to recovery.

DAY 1

"Heal me, O Lord, and I will be healed; save me and I will be saved; for you are the one I praise."
JEREMIAH 17:14

This is an Old Testament verse from the Bible that lets us know that only God can truly heal and save. No one else can do the job that God can and has done in our bodies. Healing is supposed to flow to us and through us. It comes from God and God alone. Healing is what God has given to us and as we accept and receive healing in our daily lives God becomes more and more real to us each day. The law of life that is in Christ Jesus dominates the law of sin and death. Sickness and disease cannot dominate our fleshly body when the law of life lives in us. This law of life permeates our very being and causes us to live above this world. Paul declared I am dead to the world and the world is dead to me. Therefore, this law of life that lives in us destroys diseases and germs on contact. We have the ZOE LIFE on the inside of us. It causes us to live a totally different life than the walk of this world. As he was in this world so are we. Sickness and disease did not hinder his walk. In him was light there was no darkness at all. THINK ABOUT IT.

DAY 2

*"Is anyone among you sick? Let
them call the elders of the church
to pray over them and anoint them
with oil in the name of the Lord. And
the prayer of faith will save the sick;
and the Lord will raise them up. If
they have committed sin it will be
forgiven them."*
JAMES 5:14-15

James asked the question, is any sick
among you? He did not expect every
hand in the place to go up. The reason he
asked is there any sick is because there
should not have been any sick. It was
a sarcastic question. There should not
have been one feeble one among them.
When they came out of Egypt there was
not one feeble one amongst all their
tribes. God was with them. They had a
pillow of cloud by day and a pillow of fire
by night, but he wanted them to know
that sickness did not belong amongst

them, so he asked the question, so they could get help from the Elders to be well.

DAY 3

"He said if you listen carefully to the Lord your God and do what is right in His eyes, if you pay attention to his commands and keep all his decrees, I will not bring on you any of the diseases I brought on the Egyptians, for I am the Lord who heals you."
EXODUS 15:26

This is another Old Testament quote that if you do not interpret it correctly you will think God is the author of sickness and disease, but that is truly and simply not so. God didn't even bring disease on the Egyptians. They brought it on themselves through disobedience just like we can, when we fail to listen and do God's word. God's word is a safety net. If we dwell in Him we will dwell in safety. The word states: "I AM THE LORD WHO

HEALS YOU." NOT THE LORD WHO KILLS YOU." Say it today. You are the Lord who heals me.

DAY 4

"Worship the Lord your God and his blessings will be on your food and water. I will take away sickness from among you."
EXODUS 23:25

The word of God tells us if we will worship God our food and water will be blessed. If we drink deadly poison the Bible declares it will not harm us. The power of worship is so powerful in our lives. Take time and worship. It is vitally important to spend time in his presence. The more time you spend in his presence the more of the life of God will be in you. The law of life that is in CHRIST JESUS is at work in us and through us. Sickness cannot maintain a foothold in our lives because the word of God is so powerful. It gets rid of any foreign agent that comes to destroy us. Therefore, sickness is taken from among us. We represent Christ Jesus in the earth. As he was in the earth so are we." That is the will of Christ Jesus concerning you.

DAY 5

"Bless the Lord, O my soul, and forget not all his benefits; who forgives all thine iniquities; who healeth all thy diseases."
PSALMS 103:2, 3

This is one of my favorite verses when it comes to standing on the word of God for healing. Forget not all his benefits. There are benefits to being saved and one of them is he heals all our diseases. Just in case a disease tries to attack the body, He heals all our diseases; that is not just a statement of fact it is TRUTH. We know we WERE HEALED which is past tense, but just in case the enemy tries to pull one over on us; HE HEALETH ALL OUR DISEASES. We are just as much delivered from sickness as we are from sin. Who forgives all thine iniquities; who healeth all thy diseases; on this day and everyday He FORGIVES AND HEALS SIMULTANEOUSLY THE BLOOD CONTINUES TO HEAL AT ANYTIME "WHETHER WE NEED IT OR NOT."

DAY 6

"When evening came, many who were demon-possessed were brought to him, and he drove out the spirits with a word and healed all the sick." This was to fulfill what was spoken by the prophet Isaiah; "He took up our infirmities and bore our diseases."
MATTHEW 8:16-17

The prophet Isaiah had predicted that the Suffering Servant would come and carry our load of sickness and disease; He started this fulfillment under the Abrahamic Covenant. He showed us what it meant to cast out spirits just by speaking a word from God. God's word brings about healing in our mortal flesh. We are to speak the word only and be made whole. This was to fulfill what was spoken by the Prophet Isaiah. "He took our infirmities." Meaning he took our place at Calvary. Jesus took our sickness and gave us his healing. There was an exchange made at the cross; whether we partake of it or not the exchange was made. IT IS UP TO YOU TO BELIEVE AND ACT.

DAY 7

"And, behold, there came a leper and worshipped him, saying, Lord if thou wilt, thou canst make me clean. And Jesus put forth his hand and touched him saying, I will; be thou clean. And immediately his leprosy was cleansed."
MATTHEW 8:2-3

This is another one of my favorite verses on healing. The Leper worshipped without even really knowing who he was worshipping. He did not know Jesus wanted to or was willing to heal him, but Jesus here straightens out his thinking pattern by saying: "I WILL." Most of the time we just need our thinking changed or renewed in order to receive what God has for us. I find this in a lot of the people of God. it's not so much that they don't believe that God can heal them, but will he heal me…. that's the question most Christians have when they lack understanding of who God really is, and what he came to do. Jesus was God personified in the flesh. He came to show us God's will for our life. He came to set the captive free. On this day picture yourself free in every area of your life. He did not come to do a partial deliverance; but he came to deliver the whole entire man.

DAY 8

*"But I will restore you to health
and heal your wounds, declares the
Lord."*
JEREMIAH 30:17

God is a God of restoration not condemnation. Whenever we get into trouble physically or spiritually he is willing to restore. He tells us that he will restore the years that different types of locust have eaten; the swarming, the crawling, the consuming, and the chewing locust God has promised to restore. Satan tries to ravish the bodies and anything else mankind has rendered to God, but God has promised; to heal and restore. He promises we will eat plenty and be satisfied and we would get to praise him for all of his magnificent works. Today God wants to heal and restore what the enemy has stolen from you; including restoration of the years he has tried to hold you down in your body, the years that have been lost through sickness and disease; God says all these years he will restore. Take him at his word and walk out in restoration healing.

DAY 9

"And Jesus said unto the Centurion, go thy way; and as thy hast believed, so be it done unto thee."
MATTHEW 8:13

The word of God declares that his servant was healed in the same hour. According to your faith so be it done unto you." Your faith has made you whole." These famous quotes from God's word let us know that our faith is what really gets the job done. Healing has already been wrought at Calvary. It is your job to access it whenever you need or want it. Some people may not believe you can access healing this way but it is yours for the taking. "GO THY WAY;" You must act on God's word; believe is an action verb. "GO THY WAY:" DO SOMETHING

YOU COULD NOT DO BEFORE. The word of God declares it will be done unto you. If you are in the bed get out and go for a walk. If you can't move your arm move your fingers. "Do something," let go of your faith. What do you believe?" As you believe do and it will be done unto you.

DAY 10

"But when Jesus knew it, he withdrew himself from thence: and great multitudes followed him, and he healed them all."
MATTHEW 12:15

Great multitudes followed Jesus and he healed them all. He did not leave a single one out. This shows us the mind and the will of God for the sick. There had to have been at least one sinner in the crowd, but this did not stop him from healing them all. As some Theologians would suggest, maybe Jesus did not heal them because of their sin sick souls. Evidently that was not the case, quite the contrary. He was filled with compassion and healed all their sick. The multitudes followed him because they knew his power, but that day they experienced his compassion. They had the answer to the question "will he heal me?" In a multitude of people they got their answer. "YES" HE HEALED THEM ALL." No longer doubt is it the will of God to heal me?" of course it is." Will you receive and believe today?!!

DAY 11

"I call heaven and earth to record this day against you, that I have set before your life and death, blessing and cursing: therefore, choose life, that both thou and thy seed may live."

DEUTERONOMY 30:19

Here God truly gives us a choice. It is up to us what we chose in life. We will either choose to believe God or walk by our five physical senses. But the word of God declares: "The just shall live by faith." For we walk by faith not by sight. Which one will you choose? He has set it before us what will we do with it? He even tells us what to choose. The word of God is life. He says "choose life that you and your seed may live." This lets me know that I have a choice to walk in healing or not. Janet, are you telling me that I have a choice whether to be sick or not. "YES!! But I am not the only one telling you, the creator of the universe is telling you this also. He says: "choose life" so that lets me know I have a choice in the matter. I can bless myself and my seed if I choose to do so. God has given me advice; should I choose to take it is up to me. THIS DAY CHOOSE LIFE THAT YOU AND YOUR SEED MAY LIVE.

DAY 12

*"And Jesus went forth and saw a
great multitude, and was moved
with compassion toward them, and
he healed their sick."*
MATTHEW 14:14

Jesus here again heals a great multitude
because of the love he has for mankind.
I want to use the word love here for
the word compassion. The word of God
declares he was moved with compassion
toward them; love is really the word to
be used. The love of God is what moved
him to even die on the cross. The word
of God declares "He first loved us. "What
manner of love the Father hath bestowed
upon us that we should be called the sons
of God." He loved us to the point that he
made us equal to himself. The sick must
walk in healing in order for God to fulfill
his plan with mankind in the earth. Even
the very creation groans waiting for the
sons of God to take their rightful place.

That place is healing in every area of our life. God is not coming back looking for an abused bride filled with sickness and disease; he is coming back for a bride that is complete in him. AND THAT MEANS HEALED...

DAY 13

"He sent his word and healed them, and delivered them from their destructions."
PSALMS 107:20

The word of God has been sent to us to heal every area of your life, especially your mortal bodies. He sent his word and healed them, meaning we are already healed as far as God is concerned. The word has already done its work. We only have to accept it. Not only healed but delivered from our destruction. Isn't that amazing? We have been delivered not just healed. When you have been delivered from something it is no longer of use to anyone else. It means to hand over to the proper recipient or address, rescued or carried out. We have been rescued from Satan's slave market or domain. We have been translated out of the kingdom of darkness into the kingdom of his dear son. We had been scarred with this world's system. Our very minds had been warped to the point that we could not even think soundly. Thank God for deliverance. Thank God he sent his word and healed us. JESUS CHRIST IS THE WORD OF GOD. "LO, I COME IN THE VOLUME OF THE BOOK IT IS WRITTEN OF ME, TO DO THOU WILL O GOD" (Hebrews 10:7).

DAY 14

"The joy of the Lord is your strength."
NEHEMIAH 8:10

It is very important as a Christian to keep your joy. The word of God declares a merry heart doeth good like a medicine. That happy buoyant emotion is a great feeling whether it is brought on by a big life event (like a wedding or birth) or something as simple as finding the perfect fruit at the farmer's market. We can feel joy in a variety of ways, but as a believer God declares it is our strength. Joy promotes a healthier lifestyle, boosts the immune system, fights stress and pain, and supports a long life. These are benefits of being joyful in the Lord. God does not want us to be sad; there is not a physical or spiritual benefit in having no joy. God gave us joy because he knew our immune system needed it to help us live a longer and healthier life. You should practice being joyful each day. Remember, "whatsoever things are true, whatsoever things are honest, whatsoever things are just, whatsoever things are pure, whatsoever things are lovely, whatsoever things are of a good report, if there be any virtue, and if there be any praise, think on these things" (Philippians 4:8). You have to think right to stay healed. Whoever controls the mind controls the body. IF WE STAY JOYFUL WE WILL STAY STRONG.

DAY 15

"But if the spirit of him that raised up Jesus from the dead, dwell in you. He that rose up Christ from the dead shall also quicken your mortal bodies by his Spirit that dwelled in you."
ROMANS 8:11

"And you have the quickened who were dead in trespasses and sins;" (Ephesians 2:1). The same spirit that raised Christ Jesus from the dead lives in you. Just think about it, the Law of Life that is in Christ lives in your mortal flesh; this very life raised Jesus from the dead. "Can it not quicken you and cause you to be healed?" of course it has. I speak in past tense because "WE WERE HEALED." That same spirit dwells in you and has made you alive in him. We must meditate on this and give ourselves fully to this. His Spirit has quickened you. No wonder David said: "quicken me according to your word." The word of God quickens our mortal flesh against sickness and disease and causes our mortal bodies to be alive in Him. No wonder the Psalmist said: "his word is health to our flesh and strength to our bones."

DAY 16

A cheerful heart is good medicine, but a crushed spirit dries up the bones."
Proverbs 17:22

It is not enough to love others with all of our heart, but we must also learn to love ourselves. If we don't like ourselves we certainly will not like anyone else. What do you mean by that Pastor Janet?" you must see what God sees in you and that is His best. God never told us not to appreciate yourself, He is simply telling us that we cannot walk around with a cast down spirit. It will not contribute anything to you staying healthy and whole. God's will is for you to walk in good health in every arear of your life, so that means you must appreciate the creature he has created and that is you. We must not think more highly of our selves than we out to think." But, we certainly need to have a good spirit about ourselves. LOVE YOURSELF TODAY. "DO SOMETHING GOOD FOR YOU.

DAY 17

"And his name through faith in his name hath made this man strong, whom you see and know yea, the faith which is by him hath given him this perfect soundness in the presence of you all."
ACTS 3:16

In the name of Jesus we have the victory. The word of God declares: "the name of the Lord is a strong tower the righteous run in and they are safe" (Proverbs 18:10).

Through having faith in his name is what causes us to be strong and delivered. It will give your body, soul, and spirit perfect soundness. Health, Healing, and Wholeness belongs to every child of the Most High. The word of God declares "Let the weak say that I am strong." We can say we are strong because of that name; through faith in that name we are made WHOLE. I often stand in my bathroom mirror and say I AM STRONG. Faith comes by hearing; hearing by the word of God. As you can see, you need to remind yourself each and every day that you are in that NAME. Your faith needs to be fed so it can do its job; feed your faith every single day and starve your doubts to death. The name of Jesus will give you perfect soundness.

DAY 18

"But he was wounded for our transgressions, he was bruised for our iniquities; the chastisement of our peace was upon him; and with his stripes we are healed."
ISAIAH 53:5

Here Isaiah talks about the suffering servant that would take our place at Calvary. The stripes that he took on his back were for man's total judicial and legal release from sin. He was wounded, beaten, and battered beyond recognition. This suffering would be for the total man, not half way but to totally annihilate sin and its penalties. God alone had the authority and ability to forgive sins. We were not just delivered from sin, but from sin and its penalties. While the suffering servant gives us a picture in our hearts and minds of forgiving sin, it also shows us what the servant did for us; He suffered in our place, bore the punishment for our sins, and even the sin itself, and interceded on our behalf. Yes!! We have been made free…. SPIRIT, SOUL, AND BODY.

DAY 19

"Cast not away therefore your confidence, which have a great recompense of reward."
HEBREWS 10:35

Never cast away your faith; it has a great recompense of reward, hold fast your confession of faith you have confessed before many people. God has made amends for all you go through. He has promised what the devil meant for evil he will turn it into your good. You must know that God does not bring sickness or disease on anyone. That is the work of Satan. God does not punish or chasten us with sickness to teach us a lesson, you must first know that. How can you believe that the very one who took your place would put the very thing on you that he died and gave his life for? If you believe God put sickness on you to make you humble, then how can you believe him to remove it by faith? Brothers and sisters that makes no spiritual sense, not even good natural sense. Hold fast to your faith he will give you "DOUBLE FOR YOUR TROUBLE."

DAY 20

"Who his own self bare our sins in his own body on the tree, that we being dead to sins, should live unto righteousness; by whose stripes ye were healed."
1 PETER 2:24

By whose stripes we WERE healed, Wow! I love this past tense which means we are already healed. We must get in agreement with God and believe what has been written. What about you?" Are you in agreement with what God has said about you? He said ye were healed. There has to be absolutely no argument about what has been written. You must cast down imaginations and every argument that exalts itself against the knowledge of God, bringing your mind into the obedience of Christ. Who's on the Lord's side?" You will always have the opportunity to resist the devil in your life one time or another. Choose life that you and your seed may live. "Which will you choose?"

DAY 21

"Beloved I wish above all things that thou mayest prosper and be in health, even as thy soul prospereth."
3 JOHN 1:2

You are the BELOVED, this is what John said about us as believer's; the one who knew Christ loved him without a doubt, now he is letting you and I know how much Christ cares and loves us, so he addresses us as BELOVED. He says: "I pray above everything else that you would prosper and be in health even as your soul prospers." The more your soul prospers the more health you will have. I always say this is a gospel of responsibility. Your part is to make sure your soul is prospering. You may say Pastor how do I do that? Simple." By meditating on the word of God; the book of Joshua declared that if we would meditate on the word of God day and night, then we would make our own way prosperous and then we would have good success. Being prosperous and successful is our responsibility. God has already done everything he promises in his word, He has given us everything that pertains to life and godliness. It is up to you to freely take what he has promised. YES!!" HEALTH, HEALING, AND WHOLENESS BELONGS TO YOU; not in

the pie in the sky and the sweet by and by;" It belongs to you RIGHT NOW; all heaven and creation is waiting. It is yours for the taking. "You are his Beloved." I pray you will walk in his healing power every day of your life. Even DIVINE HEALTH WHICH IS FAR GREATER. Say it today and every day "I AM THE BELOVED, HEALING BELONGS TO ME.

Life Is Both
Spiritual And
Natural

Made in the USA
Middletown, DE
06 March 2026

29029383R00106